UNBROKEN

HEART

OF

GOLD

Collection of Poems

Kacey Bellamy

Dedication

First and foremost, I want to thank everyone who

has supported me throughout my journey and help

inspire some of my writing. My family, my parents,

my siblings; they have been my rocks since birth

and I can't thank them enough. To all of my friends,

teammates, coaches, teachers; thank you for

pushing me to become not just a better hockey

player but a better person. To all of my

relationships; thank you for teaching me so much

about life experiences. I have grown and learned

from each of you. But this book would not have

been possible without my heart. It has been with me

since day 1 and has helped me get through some of

my most trying times. It wakes up with me, goes to

bed with me, and never leaves my side. In this book you'll see that it has been hurt, stolen, saved, inspired, and confused. But it still keeps beating for me. It is my strongest quality and at times my weakest. My teammates and friends will tell you how passionate I am about love and I wouldn't change it for a thing. I believe in putting yourself out there, being vulnerable, and going outside your comfort zone in everything in life. I would not be who I am today without my heart.

Contents

Strength

Blistering thoughts storming my head inside and out
Speaking the scary words; exiting mouth and
entering ears

Five seconds of courage were the longest of my life.
Fearing the worst but hoping for the best

Days, weeks, months of numbness
From sunrise to sunset one notion was on repeat

Battling the open wounds within

The wind blew a sense of relief over my body
Days better, weeks shorter, months faster

But one thought still echoing inside of me

Silence is safer.

Fairytale

With a smile that lights up every room leaves me
with breathless air
Struck by a laugh of an angel takes me to heights
above

Questions remain for the distant future
My thoughts occupy my desires

One look, one grin, one touch, makes me believe
that the fairytale is true

And they lived happily ever after.....

Dreading

The day is here, knew it was coming.
A simple goodbye
Two words that chisel like a sword through an iron
plate

Hitting me like a punch to an unclenched stomach
Watching the scenery pass while reminiscing on the
past

Time that's gone like a sunset
Memories that absorb my mind for the calming

Days spent together turning hours into minutes

But sitting here for this hour with twisted emotions,
half smile, half frown embedded into my soul

Seems like an eternity.

Senses

Looking through two, into two.
Touched by one, moved by one.
Inhaling before my breath is taken away.
Silence that creates a moment words can't compare
to.
Lips that connect it all together.

In Flight

*The numbness is rolling over me like the clouds
above
Tiny patches of light seeping through brings me
comfort*

*But with a blink of an eye the gap quickly closes,
    I gasp for air.
Covered, enclosed, fighting back the tears*

*One big swallow of the throat pretending it's going
to pass*

*But the song comes on again, helping to rewind the
story and play it from the beginning*

The uncontrollable passion I've always yearned for.

Different

It was different in a good way.
Not infatuated with the bed, but with the person
inside

Learning from each other everyday
Smile forms with every look

Do you ever just look at someone and know?
It's simple

Trust them unconditionally so when they look at you
they reciprocate that feeling,
Love with the best piece of your heart,
Sprinkle a confetti of laughs,
Forgive unforgettably,
And be passionate about every aspect of their life.

Calmness

Content after hours of pain
Coming to the realization of what?
Distance makes the heart grow fonder? Clichés
quoted over and over

Time heals all pain? Even when the pain comes at
different times?

Stuck between a rock and a hard place? What if
they are my rock and I'm the hard one?

Being happy and miserable sums it up.
Anticipating the next encounter but fearing the
unexpected.
There comes a point where you do not move on
You just get used to it
You learn to live with it.

Hourglass

Thoughts running through my mind like debris
caught in a tornado

Past and future moments beaming at me during the
present.
Back and forth concerns that leave a question mark

The hourglass still standing like the time I try to
count down
Leaving me with anxious await that will tell all

Answering the questions of the past present and
future.

Eyes

Constant beating of the heart
Full awareness of where they are
Knowing they know where mine are,
My surroundings mean nothing
They mean everything.
Tiptoeing around the connection
Waiting for the perfect instant.
Hundreds of feet or two feet away feeling the exact
same.
Blue locks on blue
Words mean nothing because everything is being
said
My favorite moment of silence.

Sleep

Words won't come out
Thoughts paused in time
Feelings remain the same.
In this serenity not knowing where it's heading.
Hands over face, molded into the pillow
Curled in a ball, arms smothered between legs, chin
hitting chest
Eyes wide open, flat on back, arm over head

No position satisfies

Blankets kicked, body twists, heat surrounds
Hours come and go, dreams wasted.
All I want I can't have, all I need slips through time
The only sense of freedom and relief
To shut down the mind for a small stint
To refresh the thoughts for another day
To say tomorrow could be better when I wake up
But you need one thing to have that hope
Sleep.

One Night

The spark between us about to be defined
Nervous and shaking were the only things on my
mind.
It was you and me and the question to be.
Hearts racing, lips connecting, bodies embracing
Heat forming, hands touching, feelings releasing.
Scared for it to begin but not wanting it to end.
Breaths heavier, movement faster, beats louder.
Shaking within but not wanting to hold back
All the moments rush back in a whirlwind of
emotion.
But this will stick in my mind for life
Laying over each other finally covering the tension
that longed to be answered
One last kiss, hands interlocked, eyes connected.
A night to remember.

Love

*People talk about it, we read about it, see it in
movies, dream about it
Some people think they find it, realize they don't
and keep searching for it*

*It's around us everywhere in moments that can't
compare*

A look, a touch, a smile, a laugh all on the outside

*But what can't be seen, heard, explained, or taught
is the true definition*

*It's incomprehensive; that rush, that deep burst,
that drop the body feels.
The most exhilarating feeling this world has to offer
Greater than any passion*

Amour.

Morning Dew

Shivers occupy my body in the anticipating
moments until their face appears

As beautiful as the first leave change in autumn.
Eyes icy blue that transfer warmth like a fireplace
burning on Christmas Eve.
Lips softer than the whitest cloud on a summer day.
Hands as gentle as a snowflake dissolving into the
early December grass.

Voice echoes like my favorite song.
Skin on skin, eyes on eyes, lips on lips, hand in hand
Whispering the words good-morning sweetheart.

Christmas Eve

*T'was the night before Christmas and all through
my heart
Constant beating of the chest creating a piece of art*

*My love is asleep hopefully dreaming of us,
When they wake and read this I hope it brings a
rush*

*Making me smile the biggest inside and out
Leaves me with the purest love without a doubt*

*Beauty surrounds them with just one look
They stole my heart like the work of a crook*

*Making them happy, my one and only goal
If I don't succeed there will for sure be a hole*

*Taking a chance that's been our motto
Without them I would be hollow*

*So thank you for everything my precious love
I hold you higher than anything else above*

*But there's one last thing I would like to share
Merry Christmas, and I love you this I swear.*

Interaction

*Fighting the morning wake up, not wanting to step
into the day ahead
Robotically moving through routine actions*

*We are all the sum of our characteristics that mold
us
Happy one day, miserable the next,
Surrounded in this body of armor that shield our
emotions*

*Smiles used to conceal tears
Laughter to hide cries
Pen and paper to diminish speech*

*Time controlling us, never stopping, always moving
forward
Adapting to the sounds of nature on the outside
But captured by the vibrations within.
Mind fighting heart for air, but even the breathing
can't be controlled*

*Darkness giving our eyes the brightest part of our
day.*

Four

We stole her freedom right out from under her.
First him, then me, then him, then her
Choice, yes, family is what she wanted.
Her dream, her desires, her life.
Mother, the worthiest occupation there is.
Teacher of lessons everyday
Coach of tactics
Lawyer to countless feuds
Psychologist to the most important walks of life a
child goes through.
Wife of love, the most precious gift this world has to
offer.

One Game

Passion forming with every tighten of the lace

Years of the same routine perfected today.
Rituals that are practiced and shared behind locker
room doors.
Actions that are defined as the norm within the team

Replaying the past of one game, one play, one
second that has triggered one year of training
against that one team

Both shielded by different armor, separated by a
simple borderline
Sharing the same frenzy for the sport and rivalry

Colors, countries, teammates all united on the same
ice
Each playing for the crest on the front of the jersey
and sticking up for every name on the back

Mistakes lead to success, errors lead to victory,
pride leads to gold.

360

I felt the earth shake at first sight.
Hours fly like seconds into the wind
Breathing never felt so easy
Sleeping being the next best thing to waking shared
moments

I felt the earth shake again as the car drove away.
Raindrops fall over cheekbones
The heat forms beneath the sheets
Where there was two now one
Laying, hoping, wishing for those second-long days
again.

Goodbye

The tint through the back window was my last
vision
Watching the car drive away like it did a hundred
times before

Returning to the empty room that was filled
moments ago
Sitting like an inmate in a dark jail cell.
Rewinding moments shared, feelings exchanged,
nights slept
Harder to stand up this time, to move forward, to
live
Memories flashback with every step.
Looking beside me and seeing the hollow other half
that was once attached

Now sleeping next to their imprint, but I still feel
them everywhere
Two eyes close and I can see theirs, everything is
alright
Content for now
Until I can finally see the clear front windshield.

Rain

Ironically, it's been raining for a week
Yes, the weather is bad to.
Gloomy mornings can start with a drizzle of pain
Waking up to a light mist on the windowsill
transfers onto my pillow.
Afternoon brings a downpour sometimes drowning
my deepest thoughts.
Rain seems like the perfect medicine
But only the wipers can clear the eyes for a
moment.
Nighttime brings the noise though
Thunder followed by the glitter of lightning
But they are my only light.

Twenty-Nine

Thank you may be a surprise
When we both know the truth
Endings are a way of life
Needing to go through pain
Thank you is all I have left
Years will pass, and this will subside
-
Nothing will matter but the growth
Intimate details will diminish
Now and forever I will cherish
Everything we went through.

Pair

There are a million pairs of eyes in this world
But yours halted me
Stopped me right in my tracks
Now I believe in all the fairytales
Because from that moment on
I started writing mine.

Wake Up Call

The birds beat me to my alarm this morning.
How can a magnitude of sound come from such a
petite creature?
The repetition of chirps grows louder by the second.
Pillows, blankets, headphones can't fight this
wakeup call.
A minute of silence brings a sense of salvation.
Eyes slowly close hoping to catch the unfinished
dream
But like a symphony the flock gives their grand
finale
Good morning to me.

Ray of Sunshine

You bit a hole in my heart and devoured it like your favorite meal
At least now you'll always have a piece of me in you

Regrettably

Words and promises faded
Occupied by others
Desires for each other pass with the clock.
Now strangers seen in passing.
I see the smile and I see the memories
I see the eyes and I see nothing, but trust broken.

3 Hearts

One heart is searching for its long-lost twin,
Seeks it out
Those hearts become one

Trust betrayed
Boredom sets in
A third heart trespasses without warning
Breaking the chains that held everything in place.

The One That Got Away

You had the best, twice, with ease.
Maybe they were clouded but you were able to part
those clouds.
Maybe you were meant to be their failure, so they
could succeed together.
You had twice the beauty, twice the heart, twice the
love
You hit your prime and then again
But with each day you let them slip like a slide in
the peak of summer
They were gone
You wanted yourself
And in return they got each other.

Distance

*Alarm sounds, body rolls over, eyes open and the
heart is alone*
*Rising to the bright sunshine glistening through the
window shades*
*Looking at the abandoned side of the bed not
wanting to make a move*
*But the choice is inevitable, it's one day closer to
their smile*
*I take a deep breath, pull myself together and take
the first step into reality*
Escaping the 4 walls that suffocate me.
Soft smile painted on my lips
Incomplete until nighttime hits and I lay motionless.
*Closing my eyes until the day is crossed off the
calendar.*

The Road

The white lines pass for miles
Each one could tell a story of a car from the
outside, questioning the story of the person on the
inside.
    Lines controlling traffic
    Person controlling driving
    Thoughts controlling person
Passing the same lines everyday some faster some
slower
Thoughts that trigger the pedal with a rage of speed
or a motion of stillness.
Sounds of the music exhausting the speakers
Feet and hands have awareness
Brain showing memories and moments just like the
lines
But the lines always come back for another day.

29th Minute

For the amount I do, I don't do.
Sitting somedays watching the clock hit the 29th
minute every hour.
Like the hands are waving at me, laughing at me.
My heart beats to each tick
Telling me time will tell.

Tattoo

I wrote your name in my heart like a tattoo.

Language of Love

Your side smile makes my spirit dance,
Conversations of nothing and everything keeps me
falling into you.
        Don't let me land, ever.
     In my life you are my dream
     In my dreams you are my dream
I found the one who understands my soul through
silence

Tongue-tied through speech
Trying to make sense of it all

Discombobulated words
Trying to make out one sentence to define this
dream.

Motivation

Waking up to the highway rush hour
Warmed by the undercover heat
Chilled by the cracked open window
One thing comes to mind as I hit the alarm button

Be Better!

Better than yesterday, last week, last year.
Prove not to them but myself.
Do the extra rep, sprint, bike.
You are your only competition.
Wake up with a feeling of greatness
Go to bed with no regrets
So when you die you can take that last final breath
with ease.

Whole-Hearted

Do you understand your presence?
It's all I need, to be in the same room in complete
stillness and feel whole

Can you comprehend your existence?
I exist because of you, I was put here to find you

Do you realize your beauty?
I've never understood, "A picture is worth 1000
words" until you came along

Do you know the impact you have on this world?
When you step into a room you draw people to you

Do you ever notice people looking at you?

I look within you.

Routine

The rim of the mug makes my lips less lonely.
Inhaling the sweet aroma, exhaling at the hope they
are doing the same.
We live in moments, occupied by our current
moment while trying to share their moments at the
same time.
Hobbies that busy the mind for a while.
The spray of perfume, the feel of sheets, softness of
pillow
To each their own
But not us, we are one.

Silver

*Silver will be failure, embarrassment, another bullet
hole to the heart
Not an experience but a mission, a command, an
order
To go to Sochi and take everything down in our
way.*
    *Maybe It's obsession
   Maybe it's motivation for pride
  For gratification
  For achievement*

*You can't hide that look of confidence
That look of fire burning through the opponent
Tearing them apart with both pupils
You can't teach it, its ingrained at birth
Across blue lines knowing what draws energy, who
draws energy
There was no silver lining in this result.*

My Moment

The sensation my body feels with each wear
The repetitive motion that's happened hundreds of
times before
The awareness is what makes it special
It's not the jersey pull over
It's the 2 seconds to close the eyes and touch the
crest
The reminder that this is the biggest stage I'll ever
be on
The legends before and after
The 2 seconds taking the past and future and
making it the most sacred present moment.

Déjà Vu

Why do memories carry scent?
How does déjà vu bring a certain aroma back into
our lives?
Why do we only light pumpkin in Autumn and birch
in the winter?
Why do we have infatuations for 2 months and then
lose total existence until the next leaf falls or
snowflake drops?
Why are we surrounded by conformity since
childhood?

Faces

I couldn't face the truth
I kept everything surfaced
I had to put on a face every single day
Retracing every facet of the relationship
I couldn't stand the face I saw in the mirror
I just wanted to see their face.

Patience

The silence scares the skin on my body.
Did I teach them to be strong or did they teach me
to feel?
I wait wondering the outcome
Scared to even know
Haven't slept but don't even want to be awake
Have they moved on? Found better?
Questions that slowly melt my insides.

Lyrics

I wake up somedays thinking I'm okay
But then the music comes on
And I collapse for another day.

Shredding

I am absolutely heartbroken
Shredding from vein to vein
How does this hurt more than any physical pain?
I don't wish it upon my worst enemy
But then I see the reflection and realize that's me.

Reality

*There are no ears worthy to understand the
magnitude of a word that describes their reason for
being*
> *I've memorized every crevice*
> *Every freckle*
> *Every dimple*
> *Every scar*

*I have to live with the fact that the one person who
started this fire in my heart that will never burn out,
I will not spend forever with.*

Taxi

They reached for another's hand
and closed the space between their fingers
Where mine used to land
and in that moment
We fell like quicksand.

More Distance

My heart lies lonely between the cracked dry skin in October.
The struggle of miles getting the best of me while the leaves are changing.
The organ aches with every beat, trying to contain its rhythm.
Stillness surrounds me on the exterior but the pain within reminds me I'm alive.
Hope carries me
Till the last grain of sand seeps through the hourglass
And my heart becomes whole again.

Art

You enclosed an everlasting smile on my face
Lit a match on my soul
That burned forever in my heart

Unfaithful

The choices we make

Have an effect on people

No matter the circumstance

They will realize

They will do it again

But karma will eventually set in.

Scars

Scars tell their own story.
They start soft and sensitive to every touch
But then restores itself through every crack
Sometimes reopening in distractions
But forever embedded
Reminding you simply
That you have healed.

Letters

I've written letters that went unsent
To shield you from the truth
To remind me of the proof.
Every now and then I reach for them
Not to reminisce
But to inform myself
Everyone was right.

Effort

When you aren't met halfway
Simply walk away
No matter how badly you want to stay
Each hour leads to a wasted day.

Wait

No matter how bad it gets,
How the pain in the heart
Cuts through your vessels with a butter knife.
Hurting to swallow, to breath, to live
Fighting each wake up and eye close
Wait……
It gets better.

Games

You are so surfaced
But so two-faced.
Your true colors show outside of the jersey.
You live for the games, the competition
But not the ones on the ice.

"Mistakes"

I hope you have found yourself
Through all the books on your shelf.
You think they are the answer
But you are your own cancer.
Tearing your insides
But to me you can't hide.
I know the real you
Those actions you can never undo.

Wedding

Remember that late September night
In everyone's eyes you weren't alright
But I know you were hanging on every word
Smiling to "If you're a bird I'm a bird"
It was memorable under the circumstance
Because it was us who had the last dance.

Eternity

How's your heart I ask?
Is it hanging on by a thread or completely bound?
Do you go to bed with regret or wake up with a
smile?
Do you even think about me?
Are memories painted inside of you like a museum?
Or do you yearn to create a new picture?
Forever can stop in a moment
But you will last an eternity.

Scent

I spray your perfume
To make sense
Of the scent
That sent by senses alive
For the first time.

Broke

Broken bones-heal
Broken hearts-mend
Broken trust.....

Home

I got used to your keys thrown next to mine
Our jackets hung up in a line
Your shoes thrown off on the floor
Your scent welcoming me through the door.

Ink

I won't waste ink on you anymore
These last few words try to endure
Our eyes caught one last glimpse through the door
Where there was 2 there is no more.

Impossible

I've been waiting for you
To pull into my driveway
Walk up the steps
Open the door
Get down on one knee
And erase the pain
But that requires effort.

Same Me

Different passenger seat
Different lips
Different scent
Different sheets
Same me.

Treasure Chests

As the sun goes down and the lights dim
I sometimes feel your heart beating on me like it did

2 treasure chests creating their own duet
Established the instant our eyes met.

Hide and Seek

You have my heart locked up somewhere.
You take it out to play from time to time
It's like a game of hide and seek
Where I never win.
I'll just build a new one
You can keep it
To remind you of what you had.

Sparks

That's what we do we fight.
You can't leave a wet towel on the bed
And expect nothing to be said.
I can't be distracted when I drive
Because I have precious cargo by my side.
You change outfits 10 times before we leave
And you wore the first one with complete ease.
Yes, we are stubborn and get under skin
But at the end of the day it's a win win.
You take an hour to pick out a movie
And within minutes you are sleeping beauty.
You spend and buy way too much
And I can never just shut up.
Yes, everything we do we compete
But it's in our nature to never be beat.
Somedays we weren't elite
But at the end of the night
Between the sheets
No two hearts
Could radiate
That degree of heat.

City Streets

I packed up my life
And you saved it.
I crossed the border in chains
Wrapped around every muscle
And you were holding the key.

Why

All these words are the sum of every sleepless night
Turning to the only 2 things I trust
A blank page and a pen
That creates magic.

Me

Her strength seems inhumane
She wears it on her sleeve
Born in the wrong era
Where nobody understands
The kind of love she was destined to find
That passion is too intense
For any lifeline.

Mirror

I've never seen someone look in the mirror so much
And fail to see the reflection looking back.
You stand there and observe your every curve
Making sure you've satisfied every nerve

But what you truly should see doesn't occur
The reality of the truth is insecure

One day I hope it will emerge.

Live and Learn

*How dare you have the audacity to try and compete
with the connection that we both created.
To think you would ever come close to comparing
with the closeness we consummated.
You were blinded by every inch of their exterior
walls
While I was the interior designer of their cœur.*

Secrets

Your facial scruff tickled my cheek
For a moment it made me weak
You were different to say the least
And my only option for a release

You were my car for the night and I paid the lease
Nobody would have guessed my feelings would
increase
The night I remember was so unique
You showed me your every technique

In the morning I replayed it piece by piece
And we swore from that day on to never speak.

Frost Bite

I took the day to try and recover
Only to discover

That my heart was doing cardio
While replaying every scenario

When will I have a day off?
Where I don't feel so soft?

Maybe I am meant to be lost
While their cold heart can defrost.

Follower

I've been a detective of your growth for years
But it was stunted between the ears.
You've been entitled since birth
Manipulating people into your curse.
You've already hit your prime
But you'll make it through with another whine.
At the end of the day you will end up alone
Or with at least your clone.

Grandma

We miss you-
Your warmth was always home to us.
The smell of Benson and Hedges
Mixed with your favorite drink
Became a childhood scent.
Your love and support
Were a part of the foundation of our family.
I will carry on that legacy
Till we meet again.

With all my love

-Your Little Angel

Made in the USA
Lexington, KY
19 December 2018